For those who are on this journey with me,
and those that used to be.
You make my world beautiful.

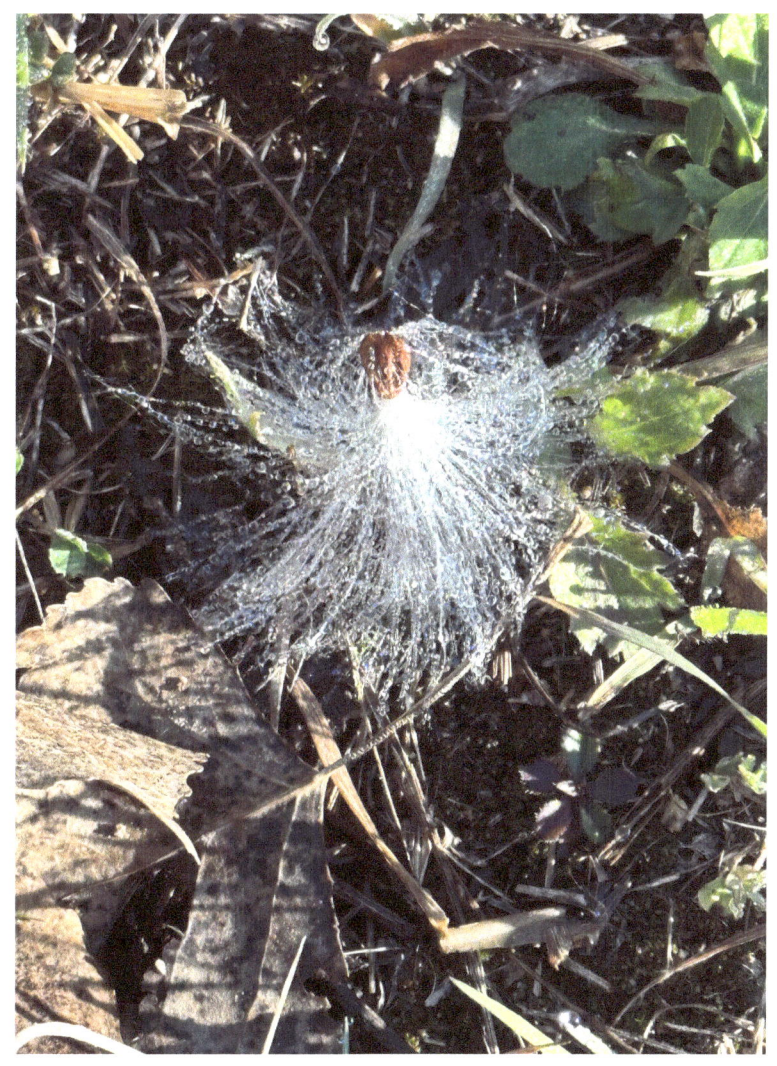

I wish for you...

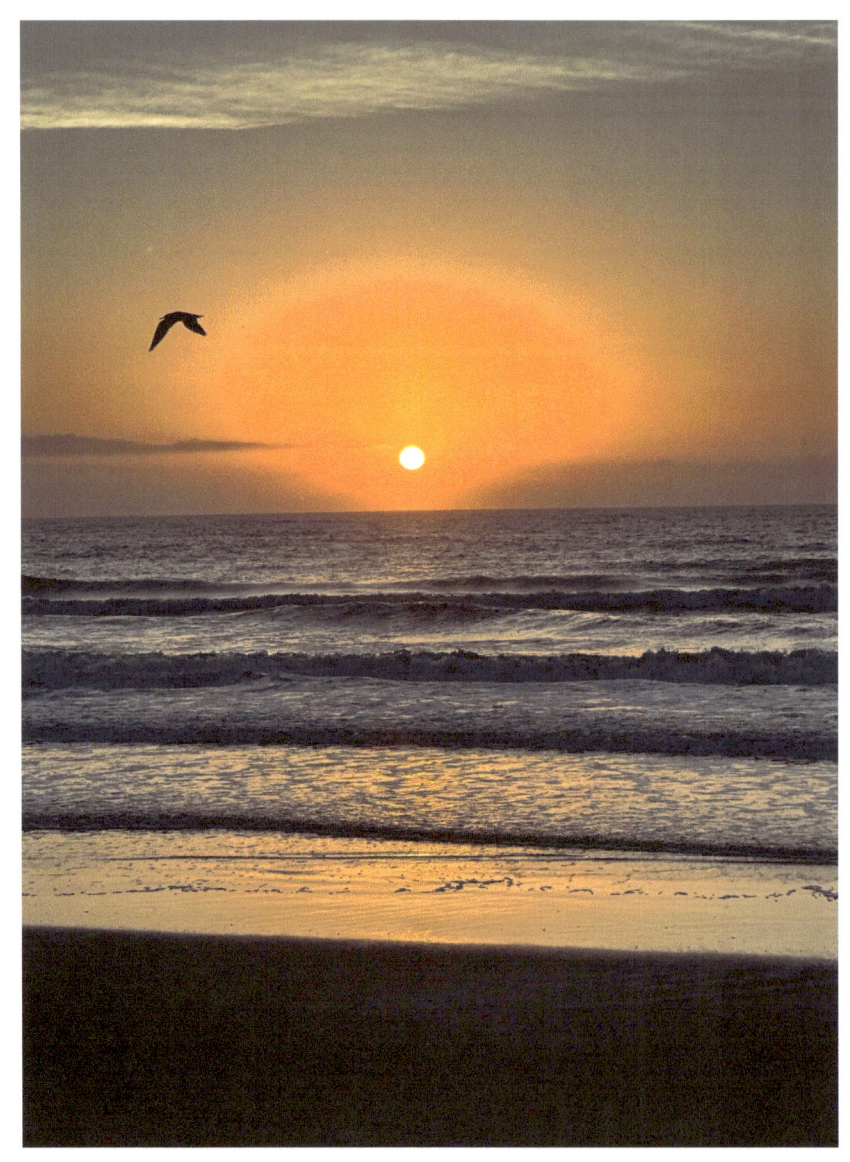

Morings of great promise...

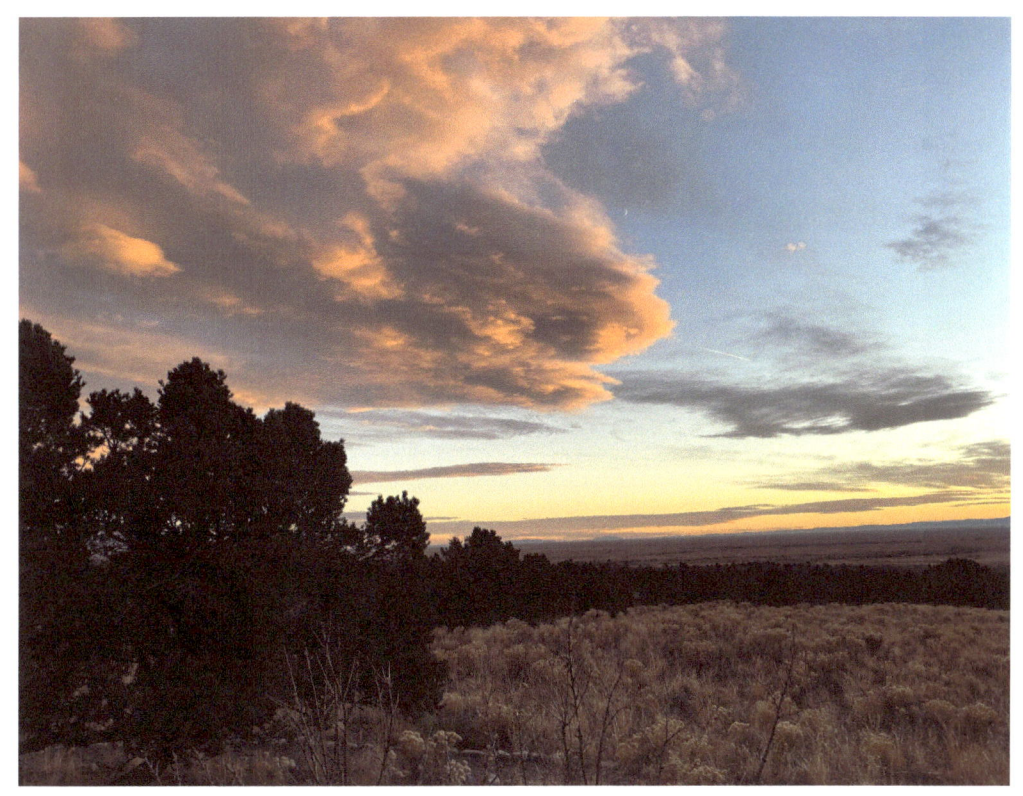

...and days that bring peace.

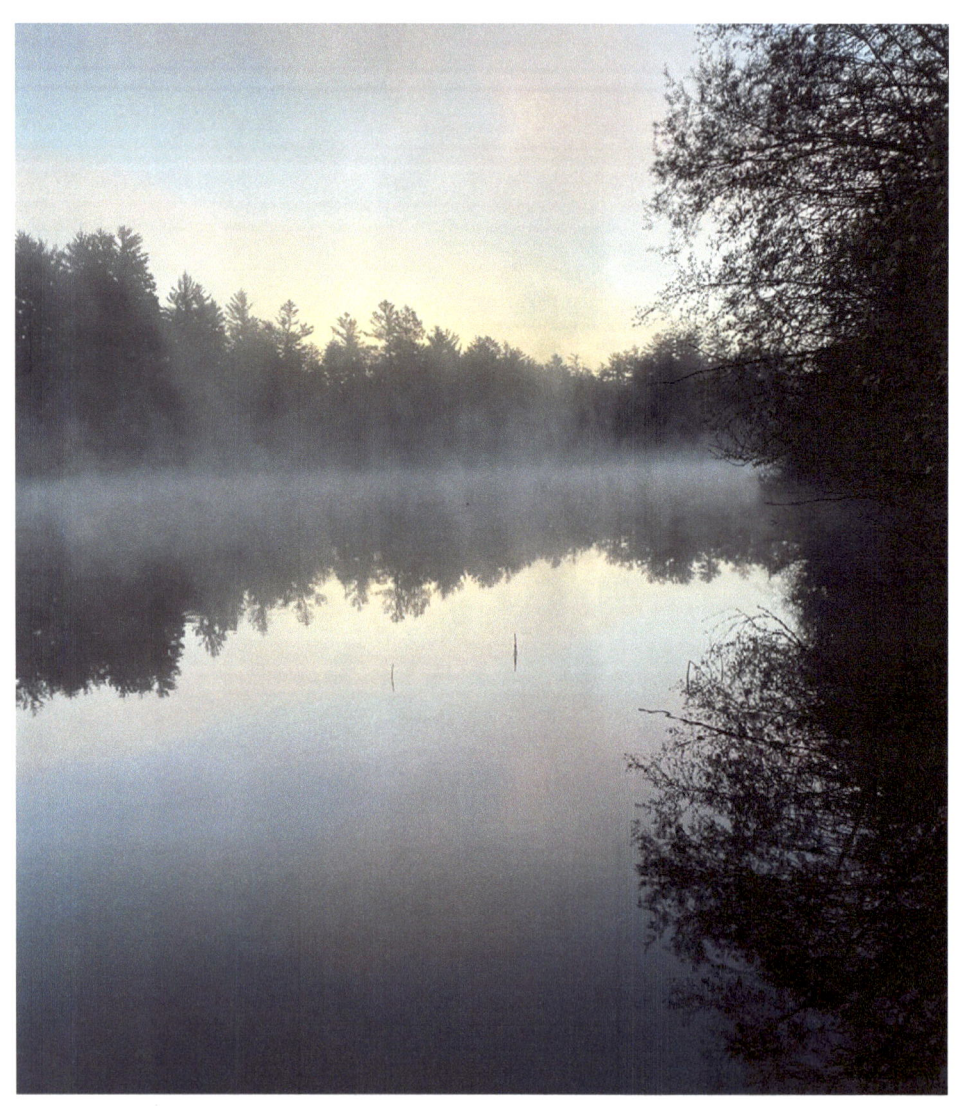

Moments of quiet stillness...

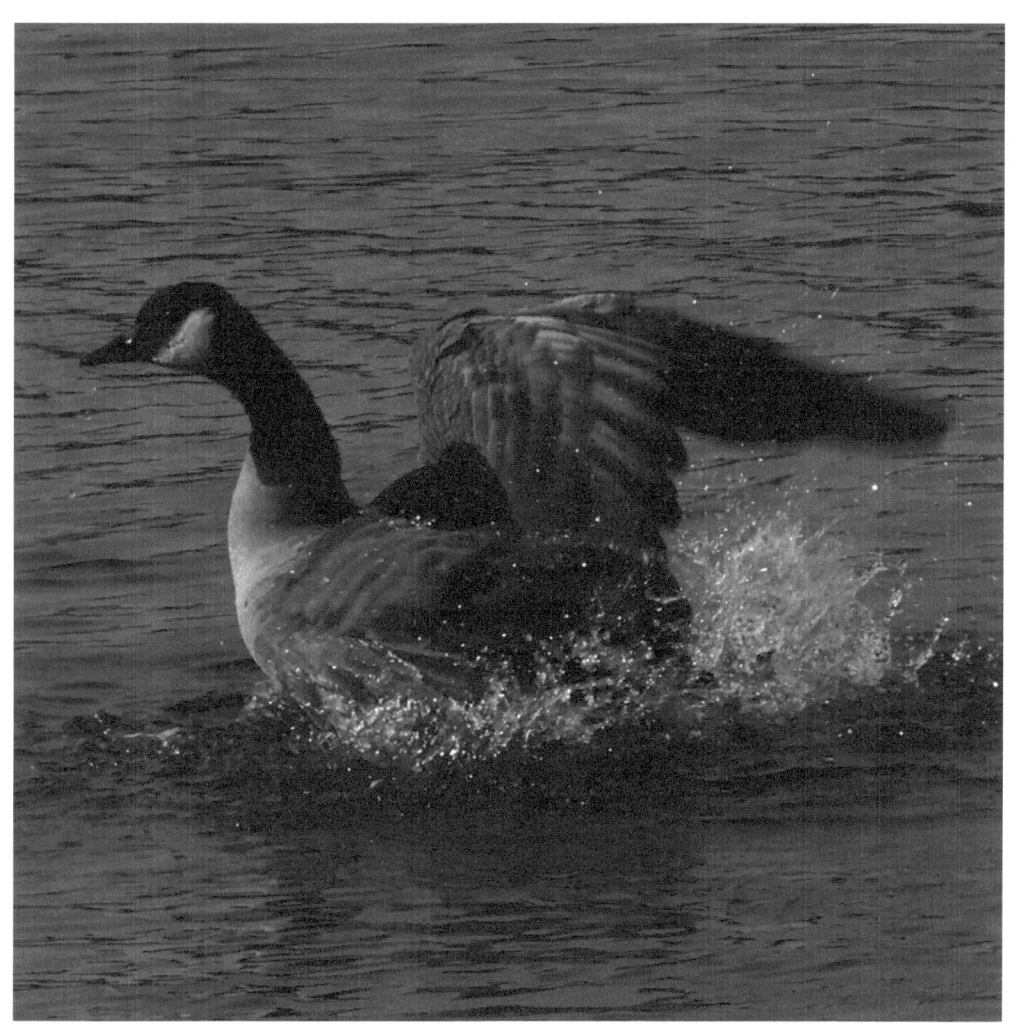

...and joy that is boundless.

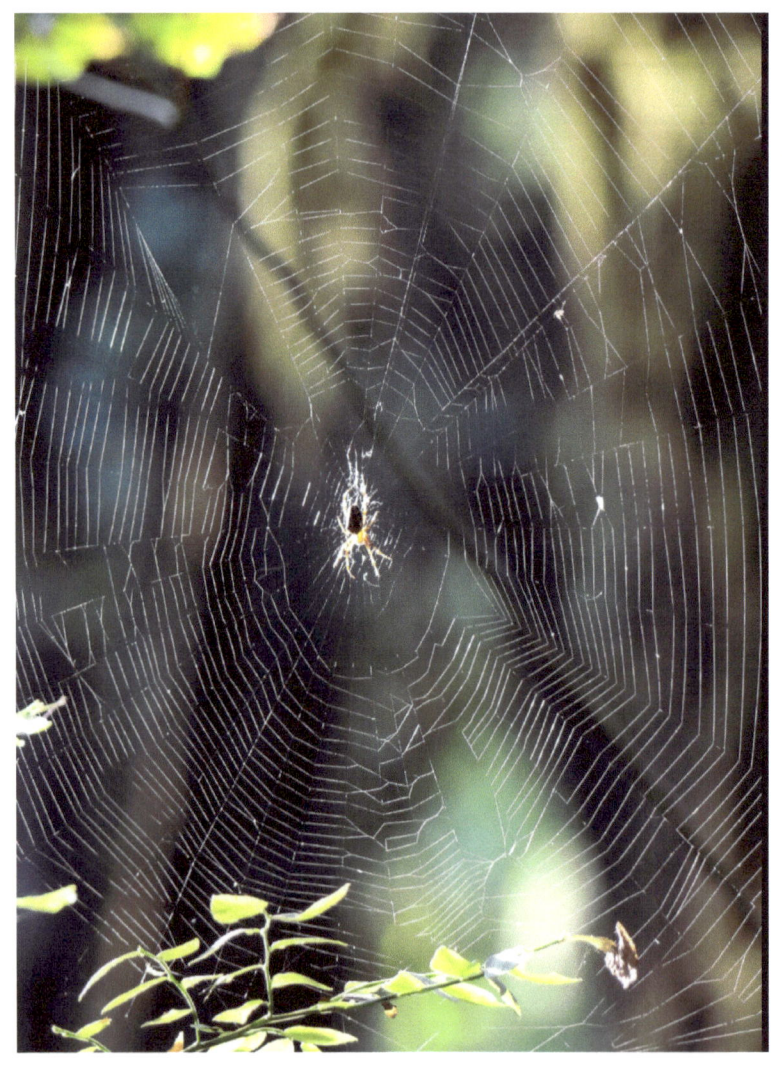

To make time to create,

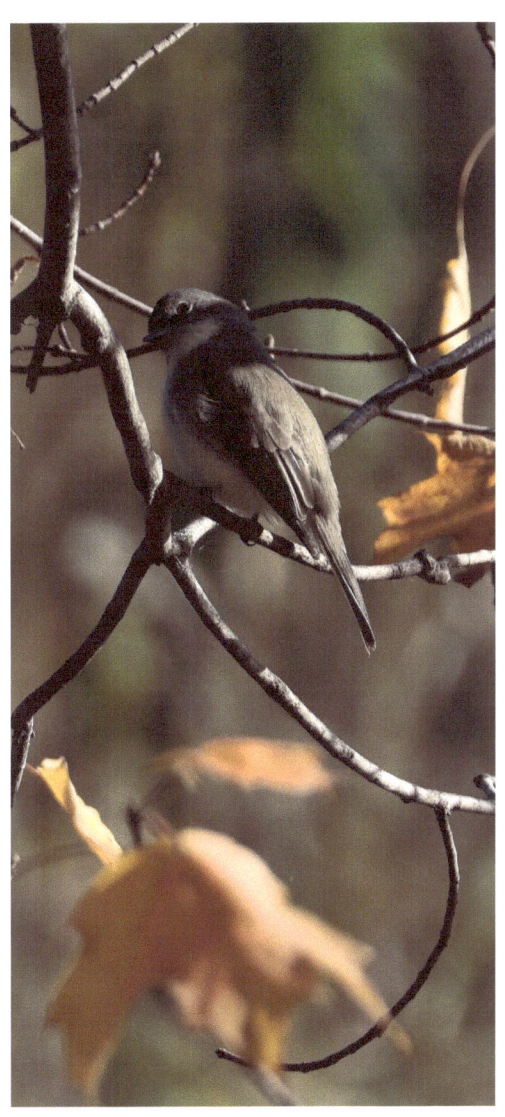

and to wonder,

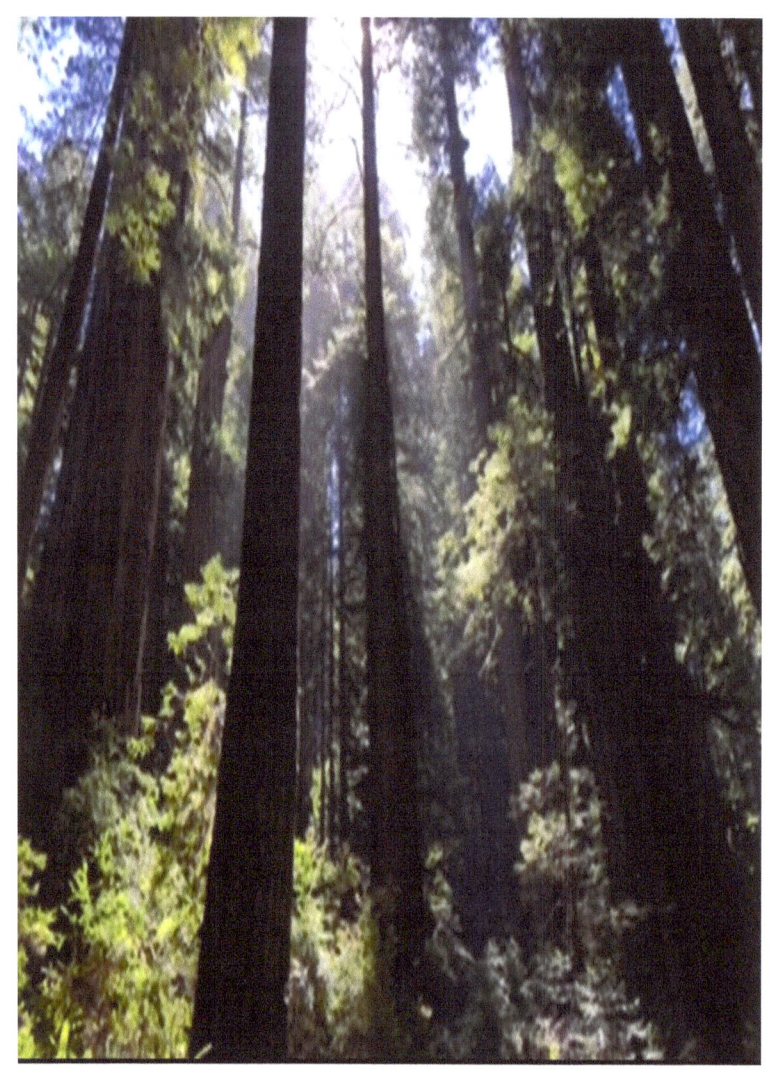

experience awe,

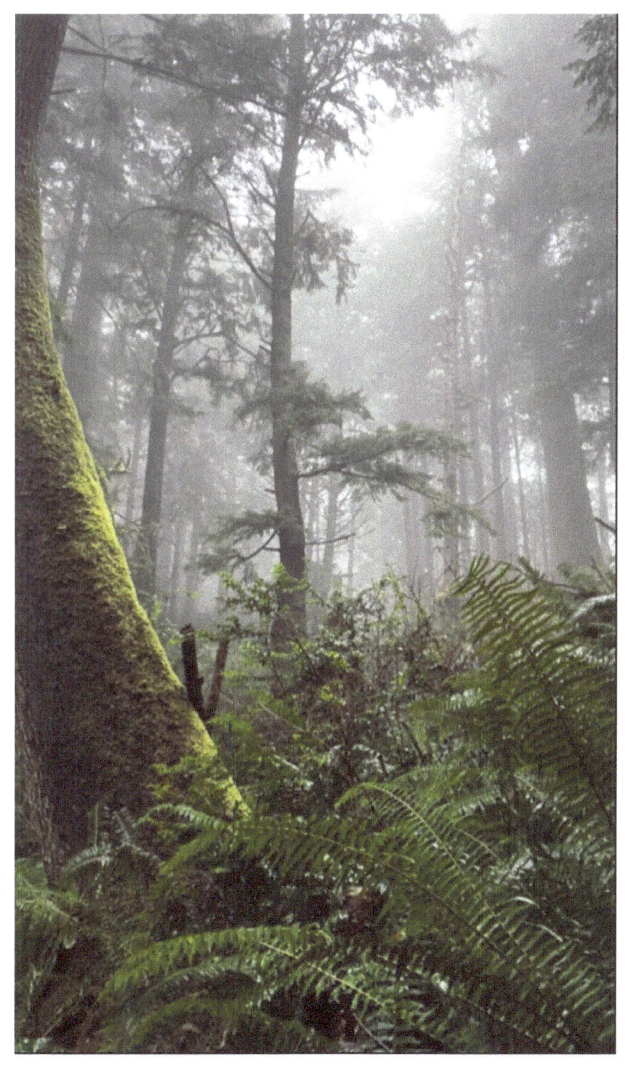

and mystery.

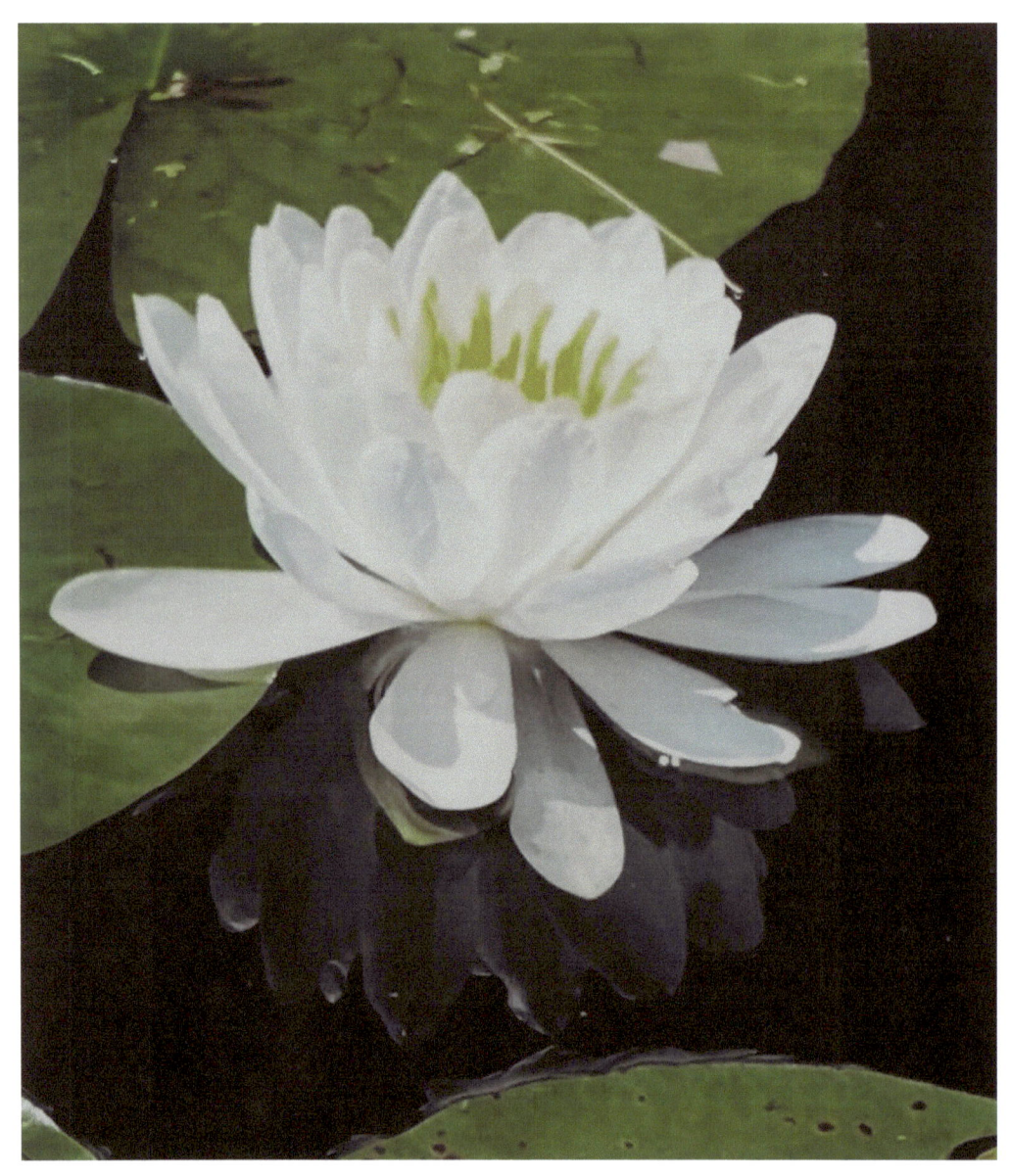

And to reflect on it all.

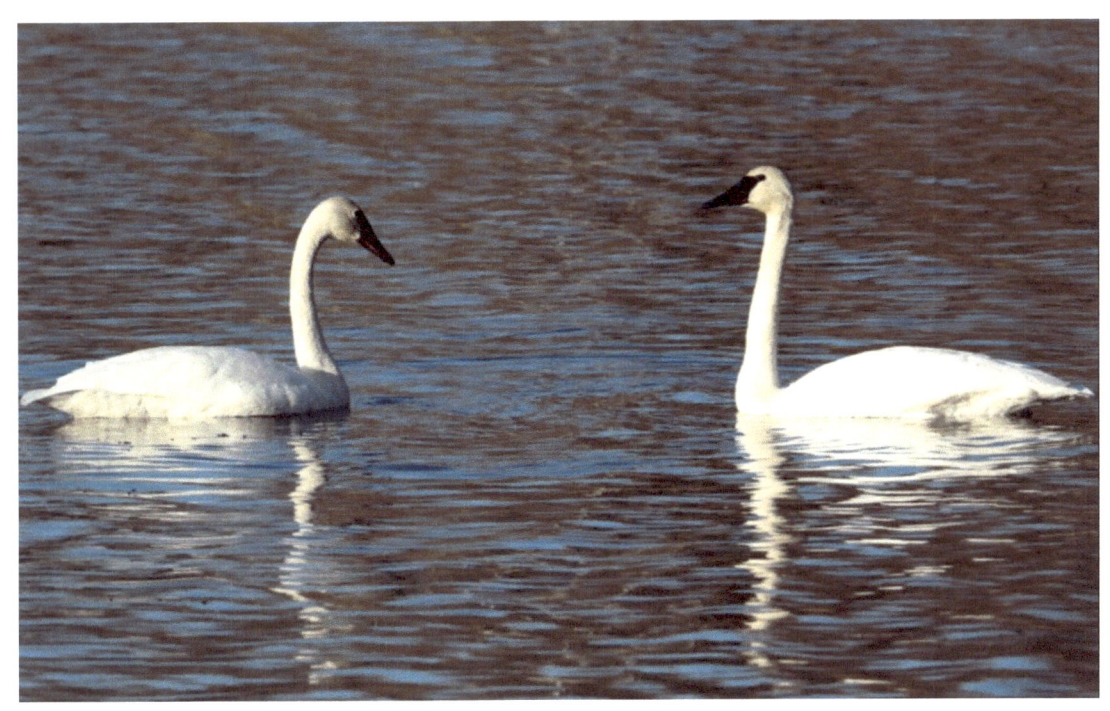

I wish you time with those you love,

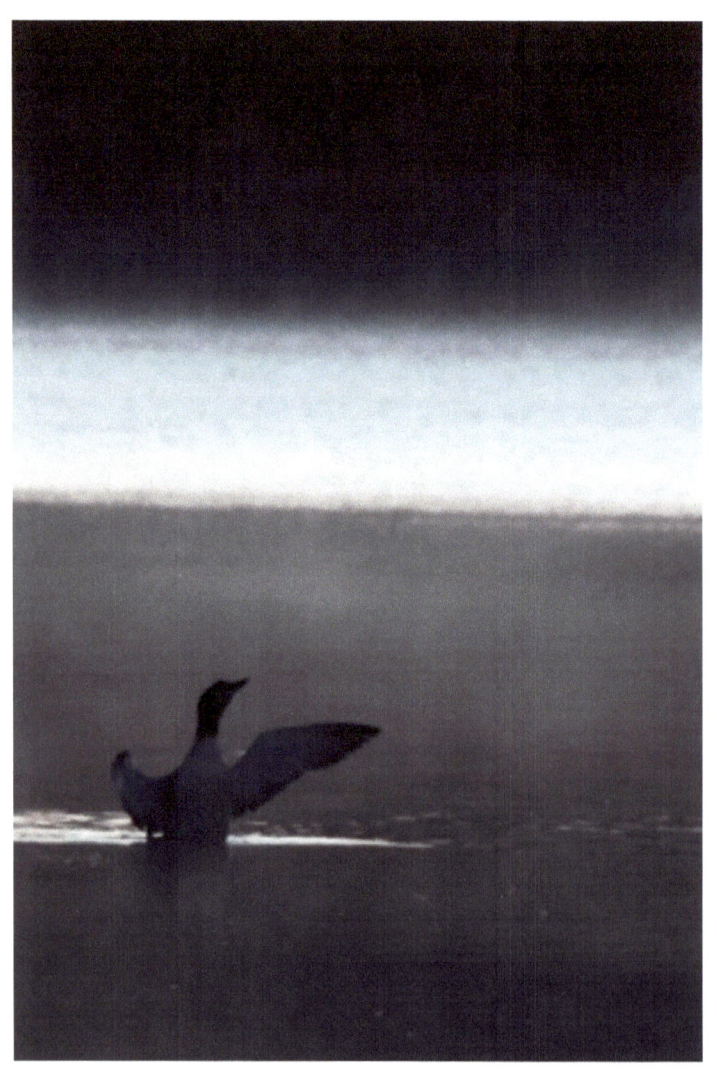

ease in being alone,

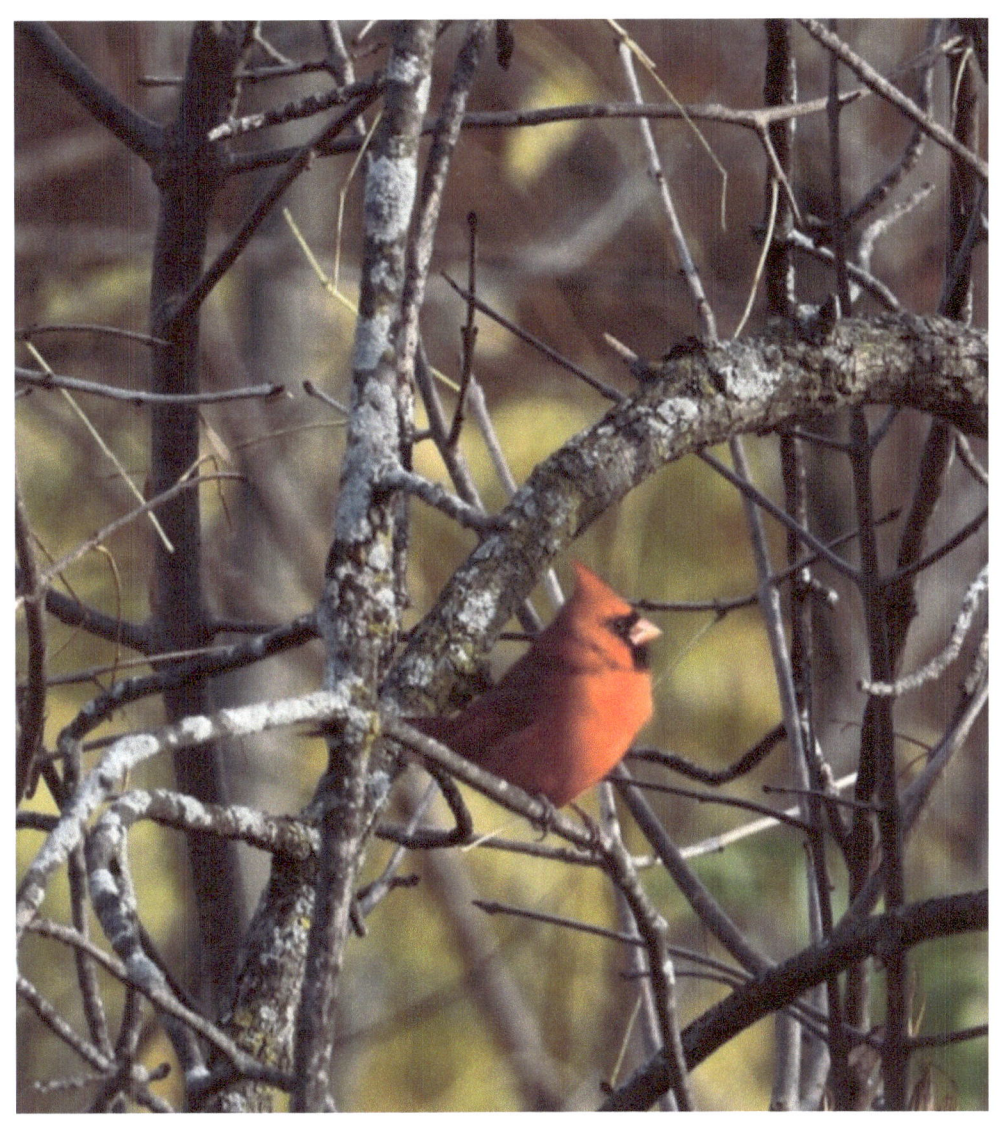

and cherished memories of those you've lost.

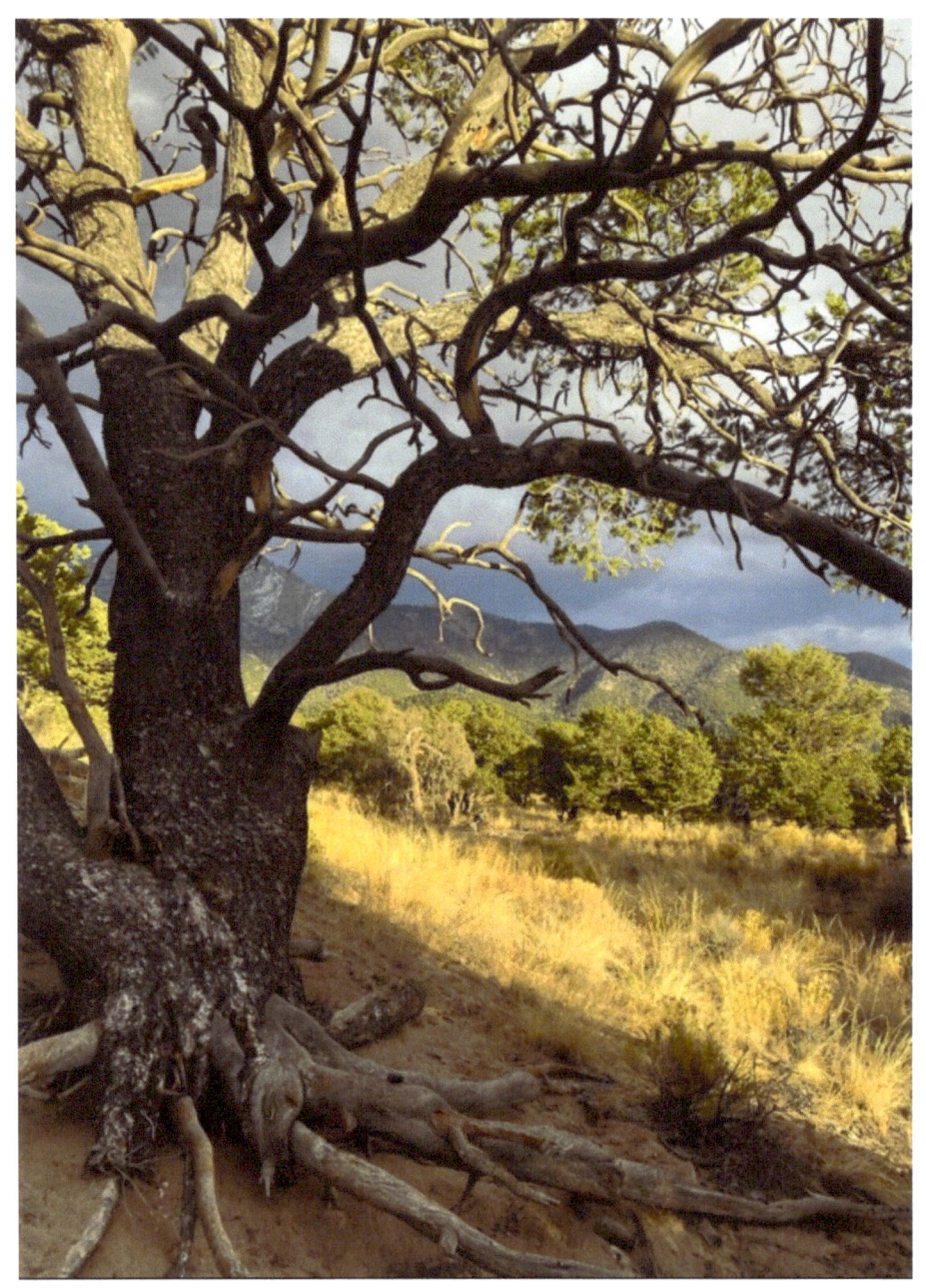

I wish for you to stay both grounded...

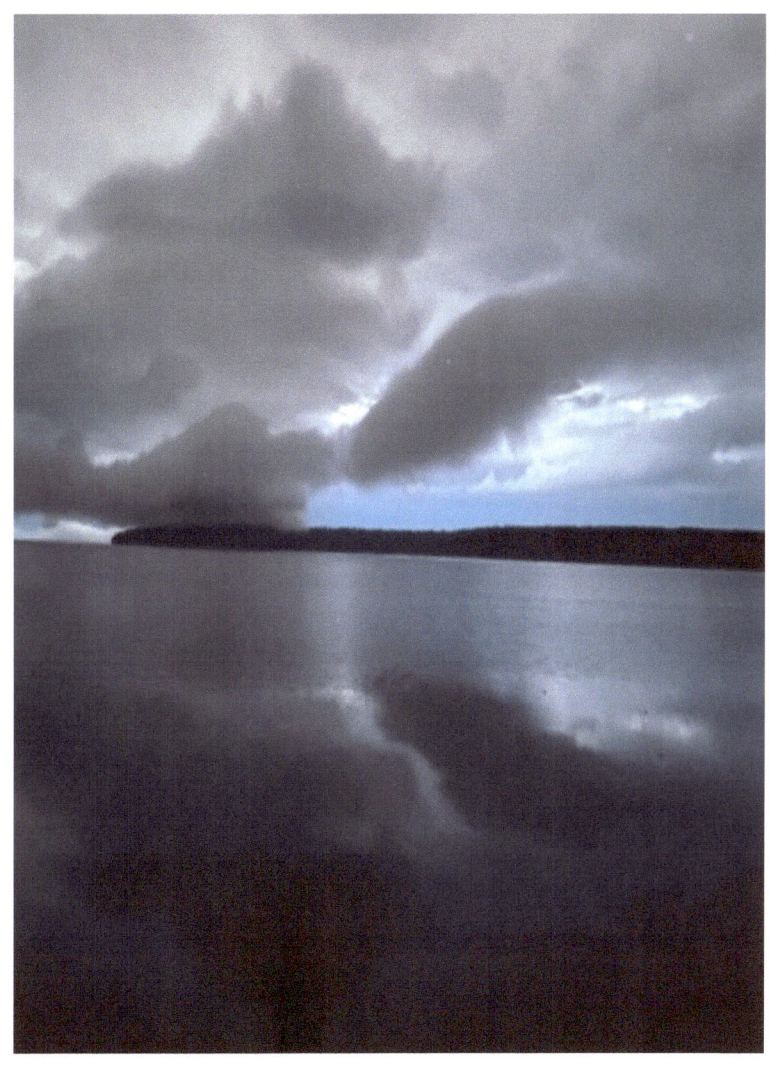

...and free.

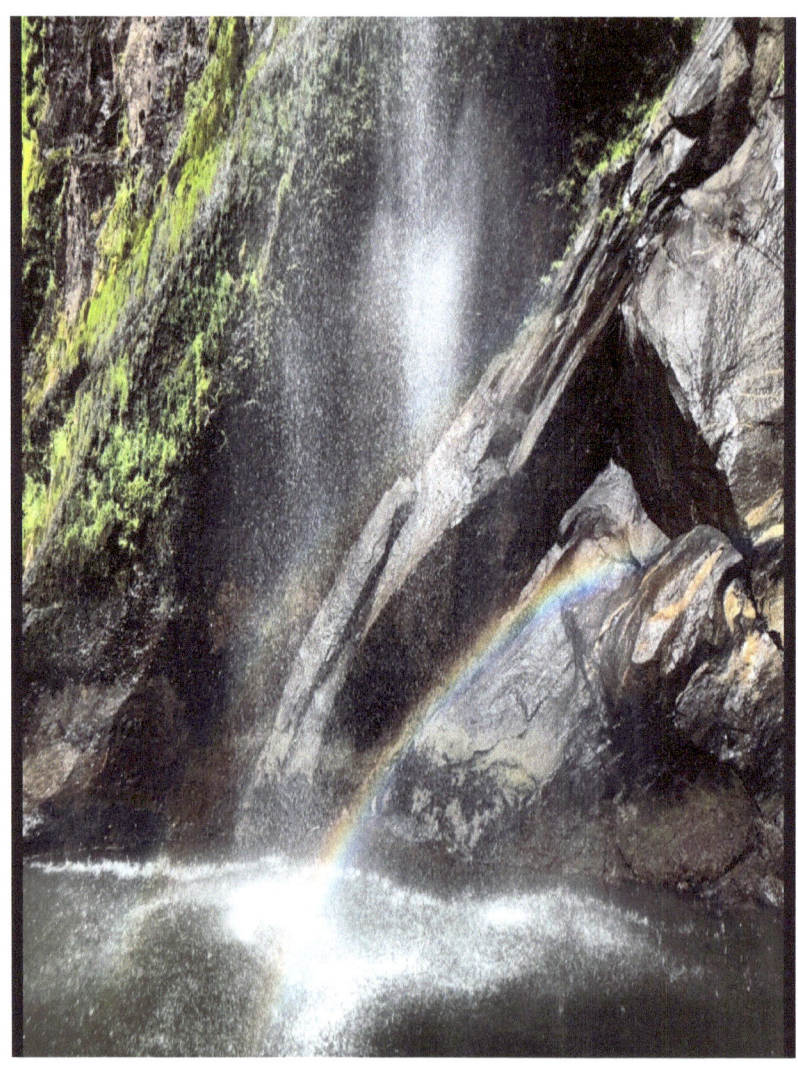

And that you always have something to believe in.

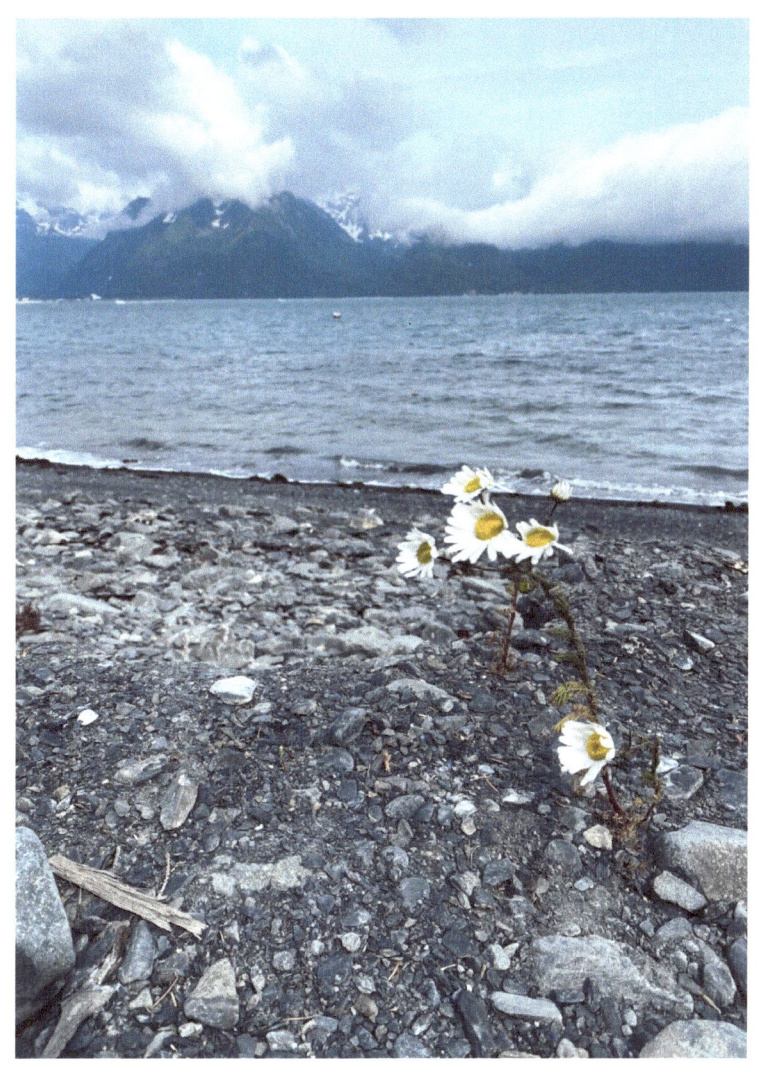

I hope you experience resiliency,

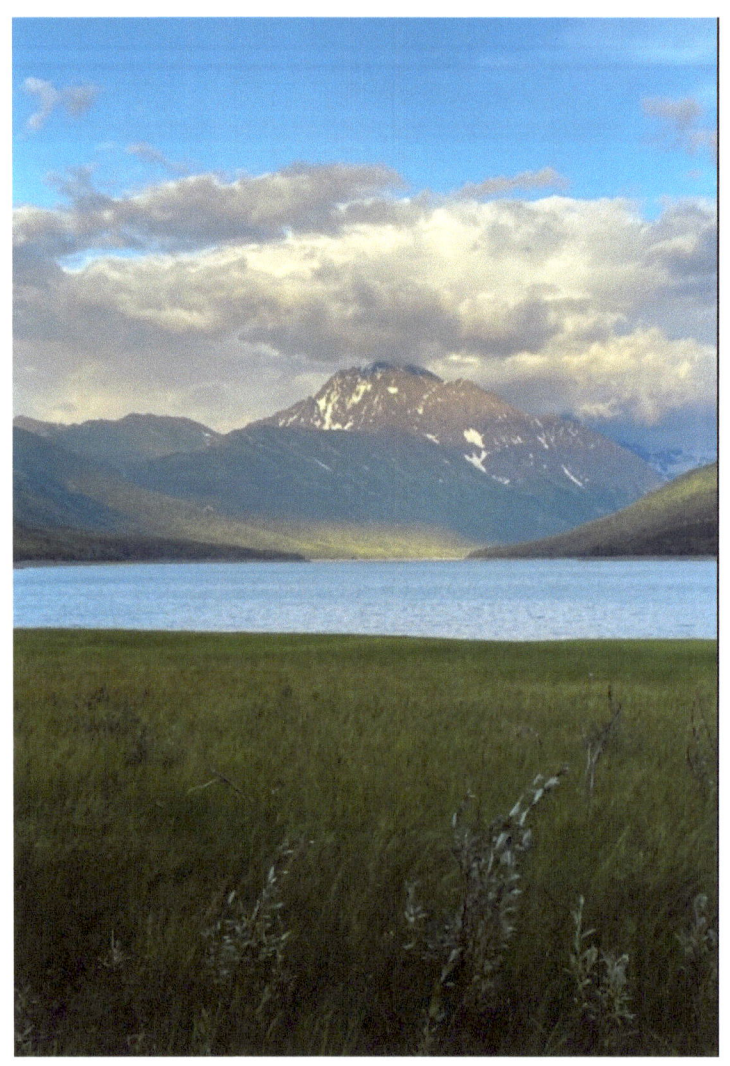

and strength.

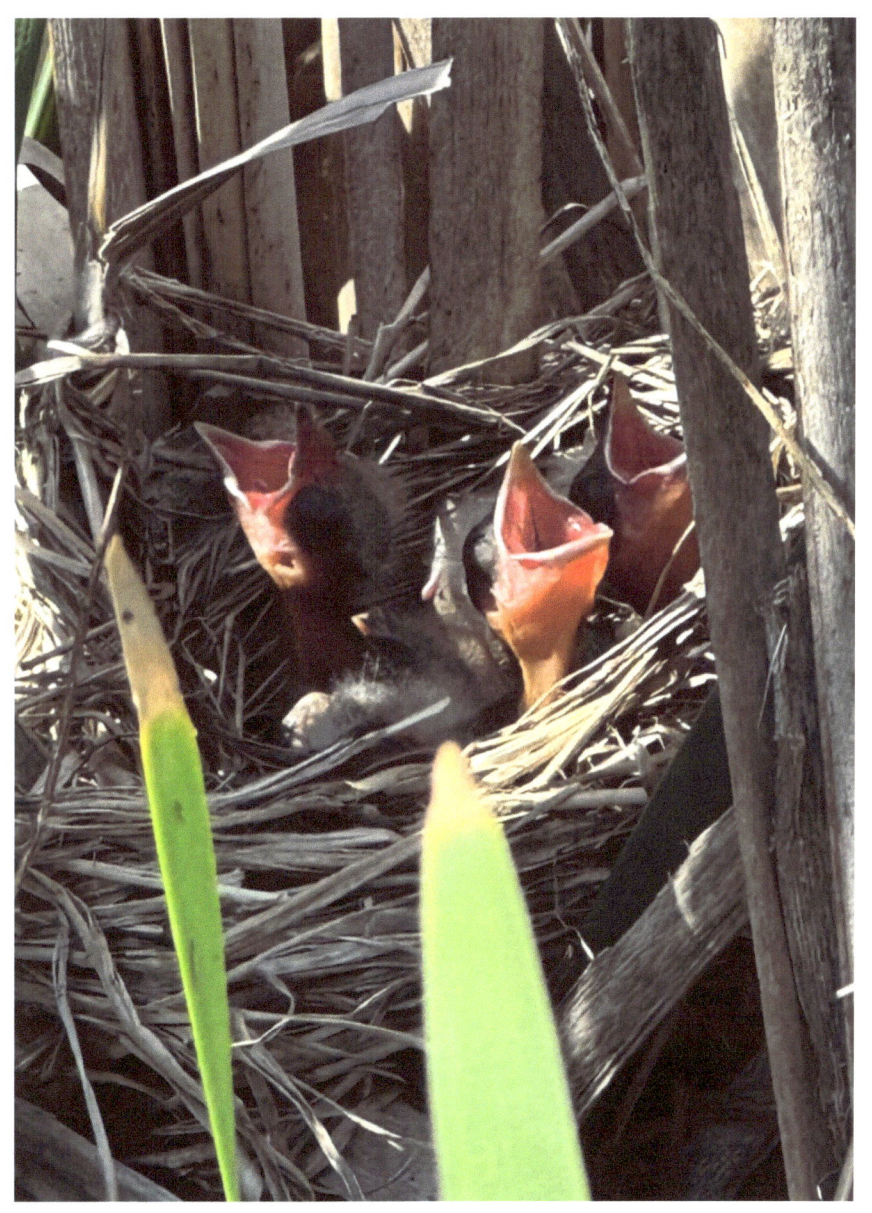

I hope you seek for what you yearn for,

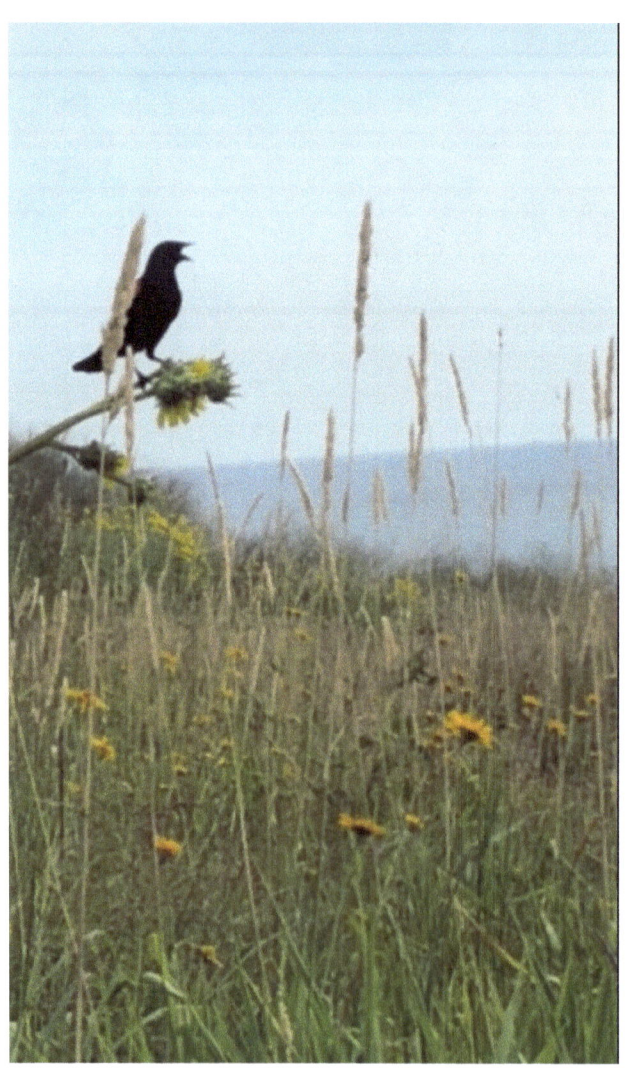

and have the confidence to express your truth..

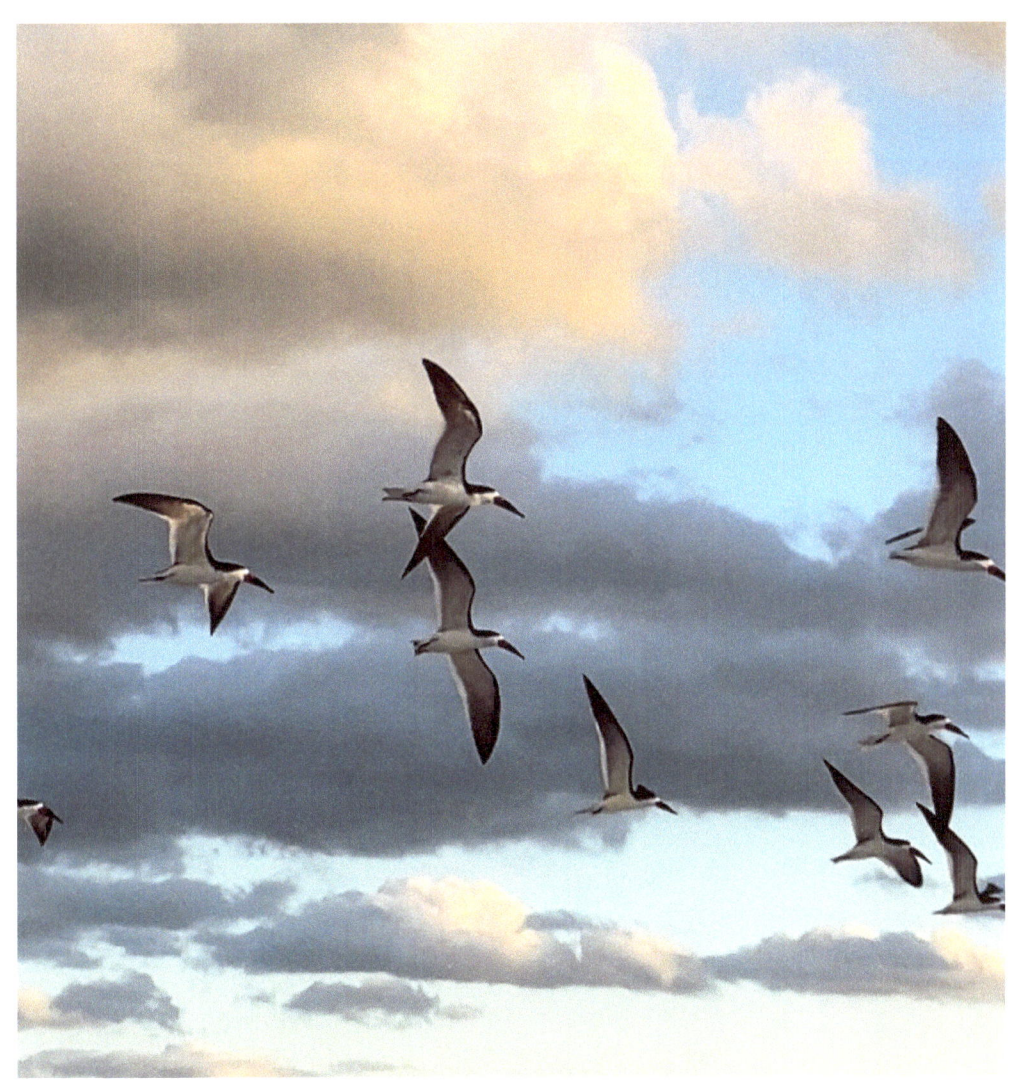

I wish you bravery to go on adventures...

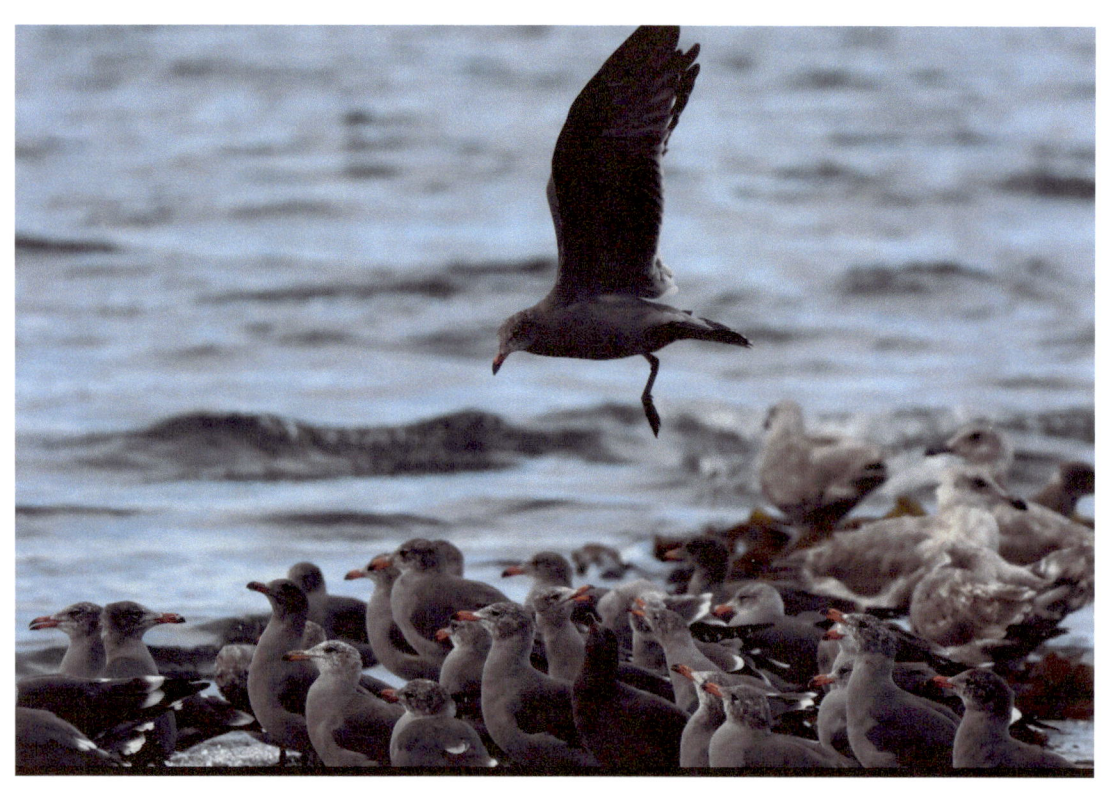

...and the comfort of returning home.

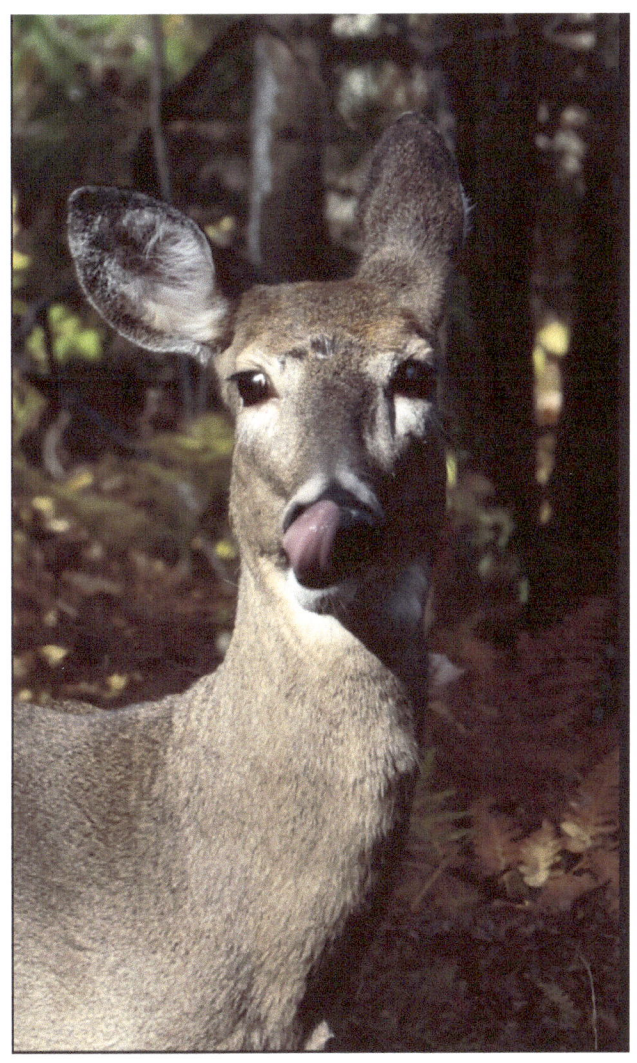

That life for you is delicious,

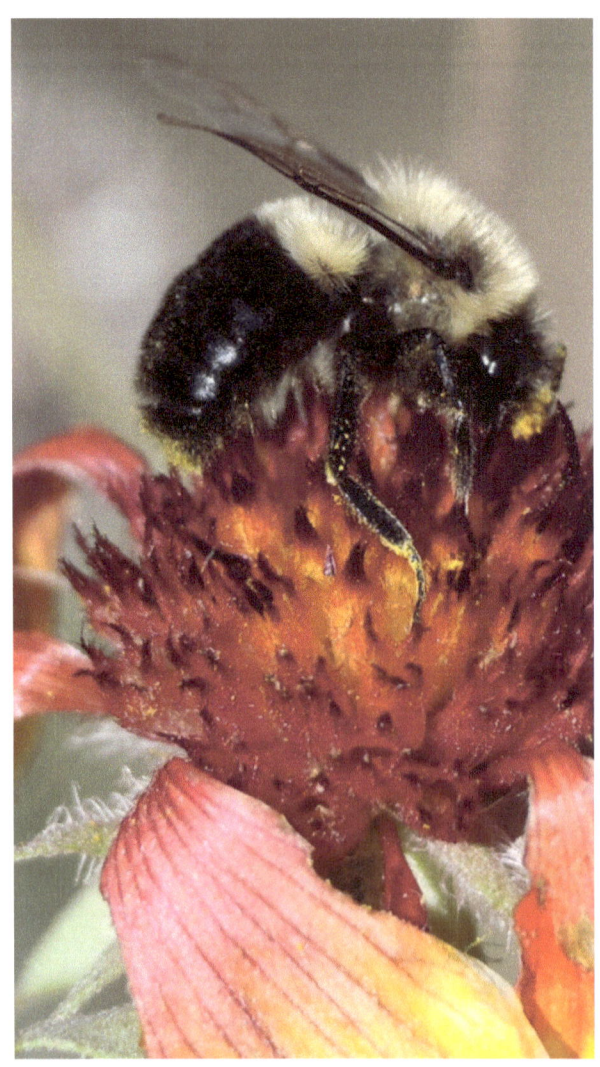

sweet,

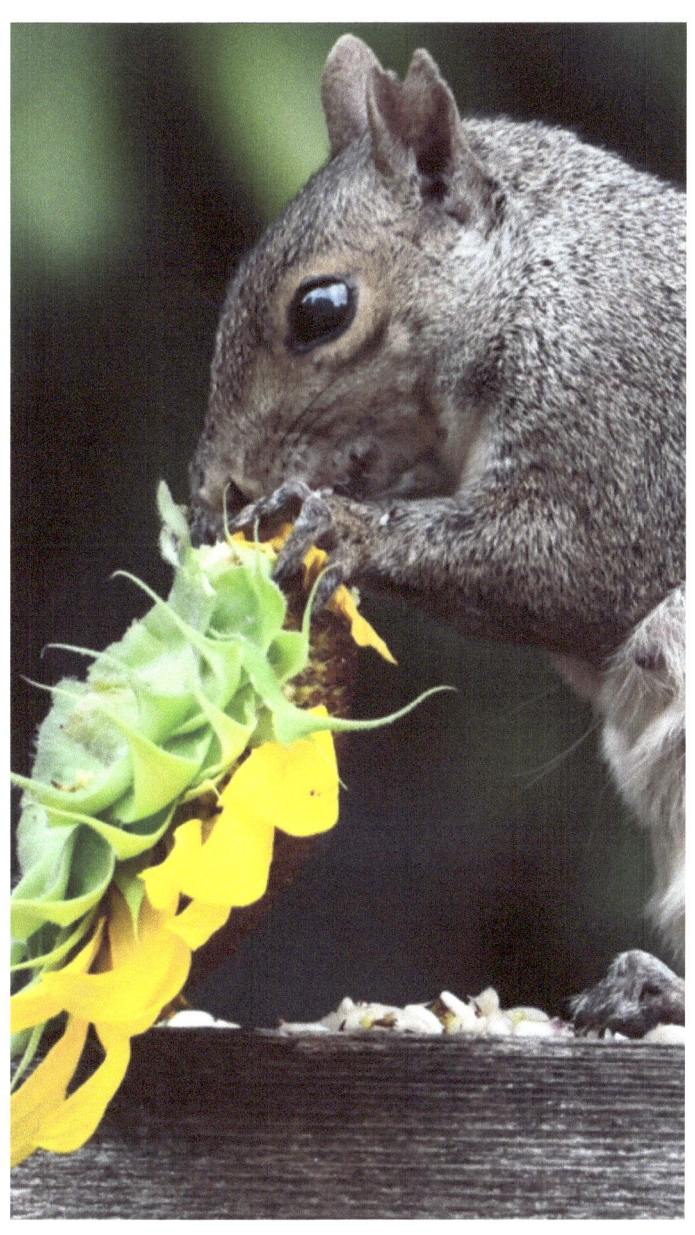

and abundantly full.

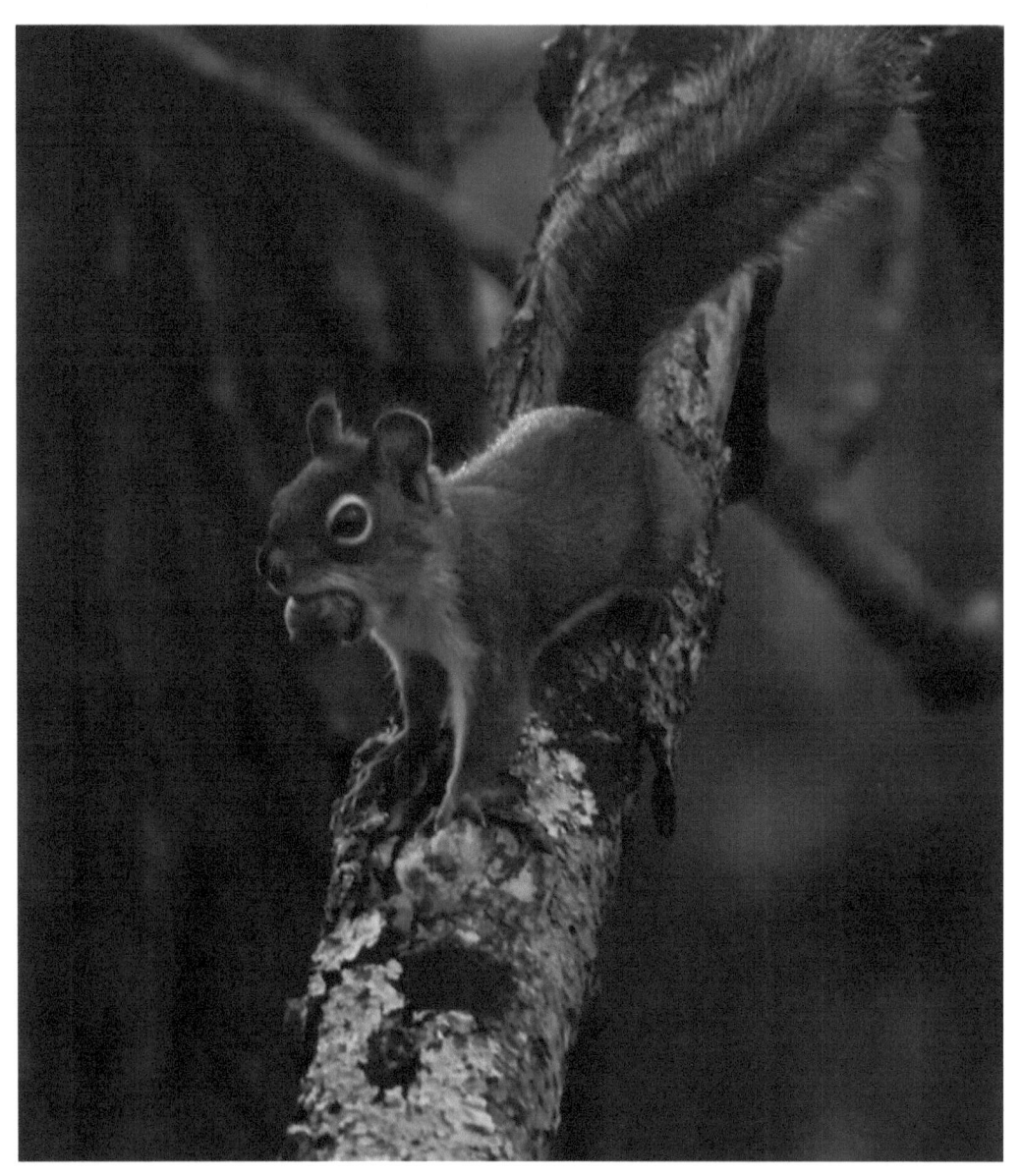

I hope that you appreciate the gifts of this world,

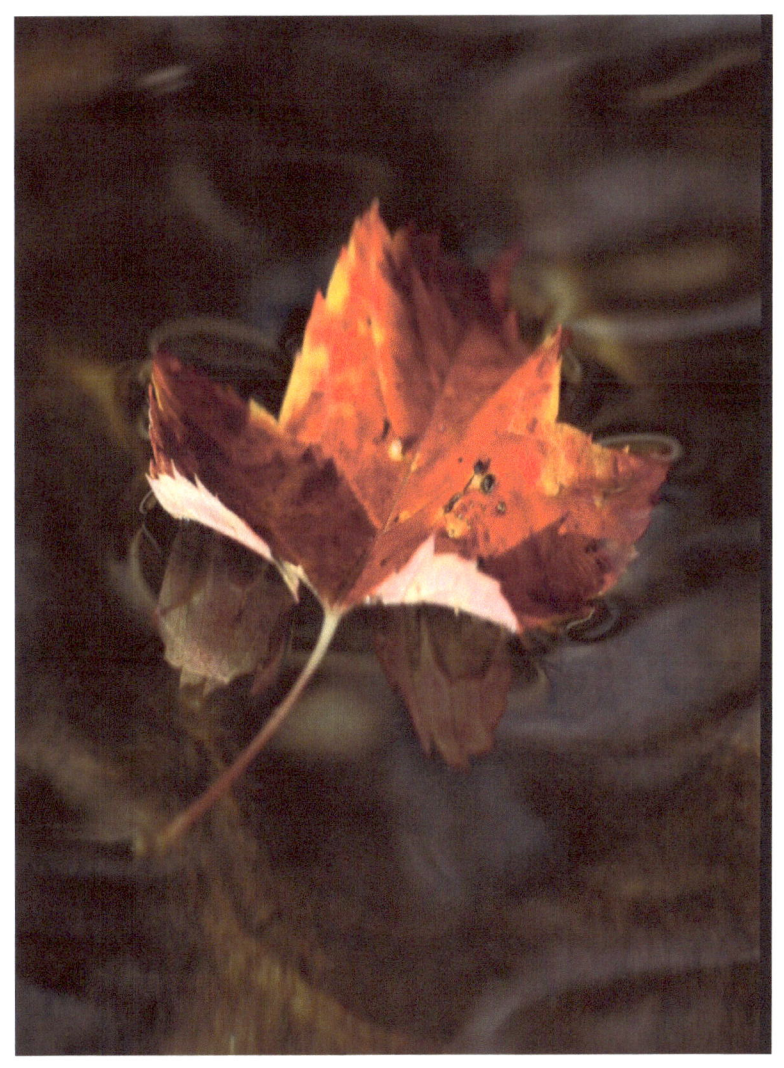

and accept change with grace to let go.

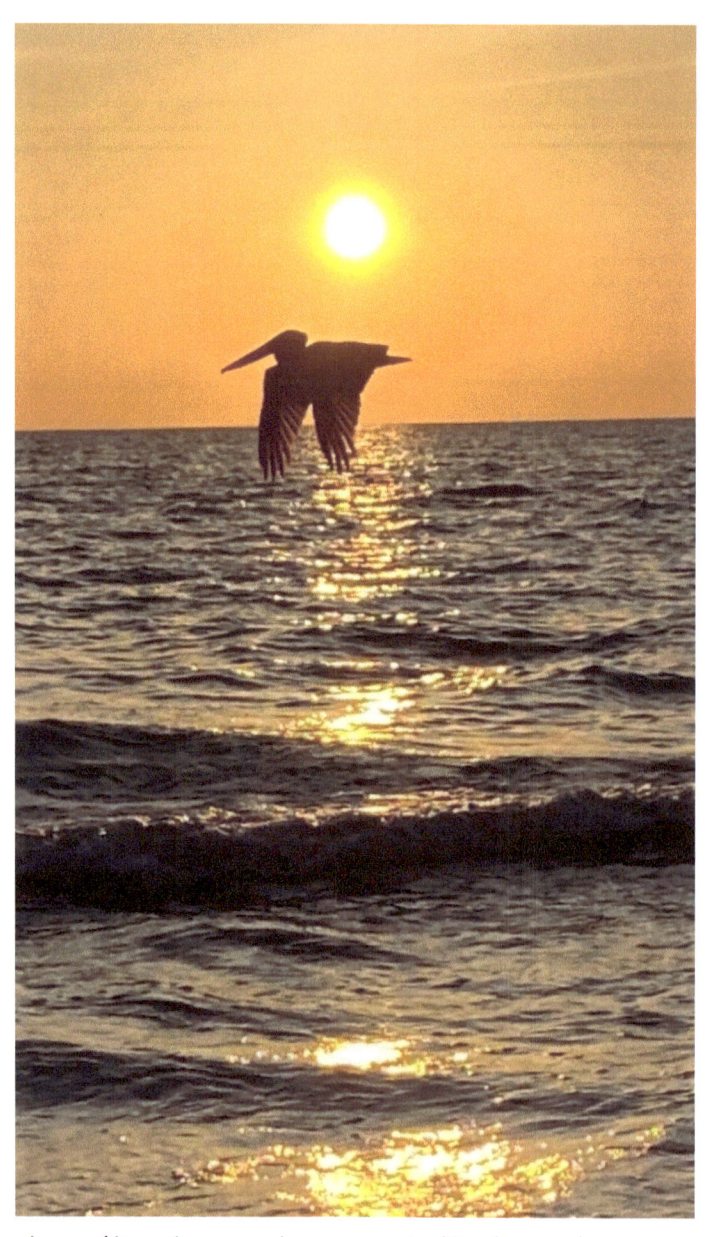

And when the day is done, and it's time to move on.....

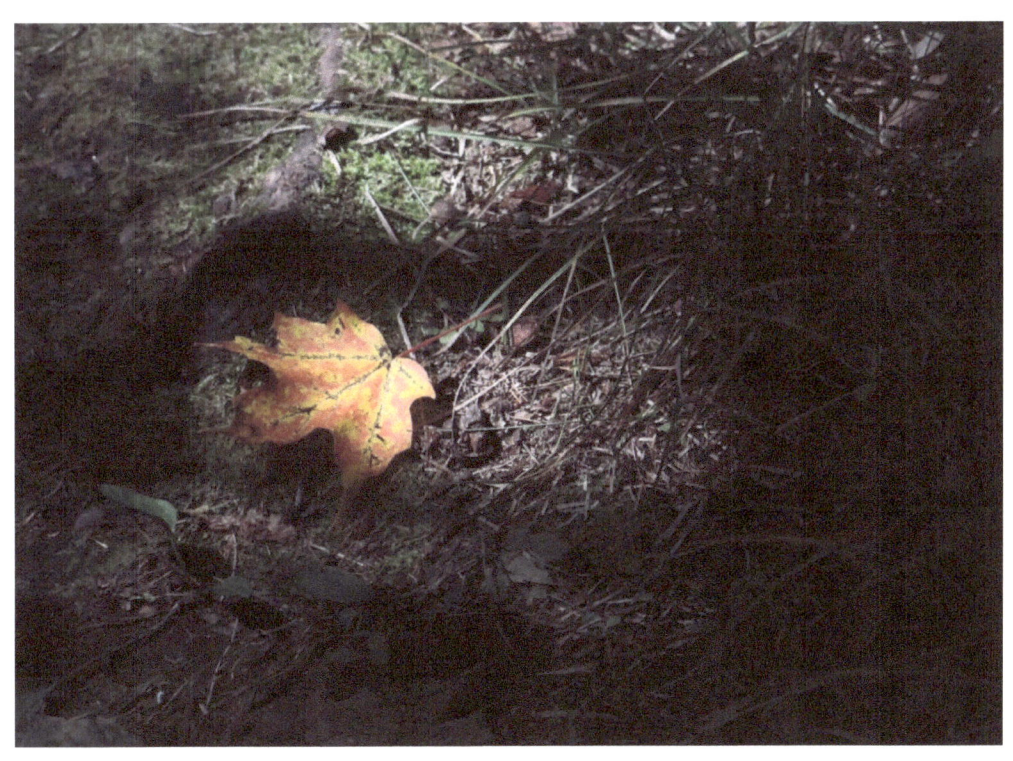

I wish for you a lifetime of sacred memories...,

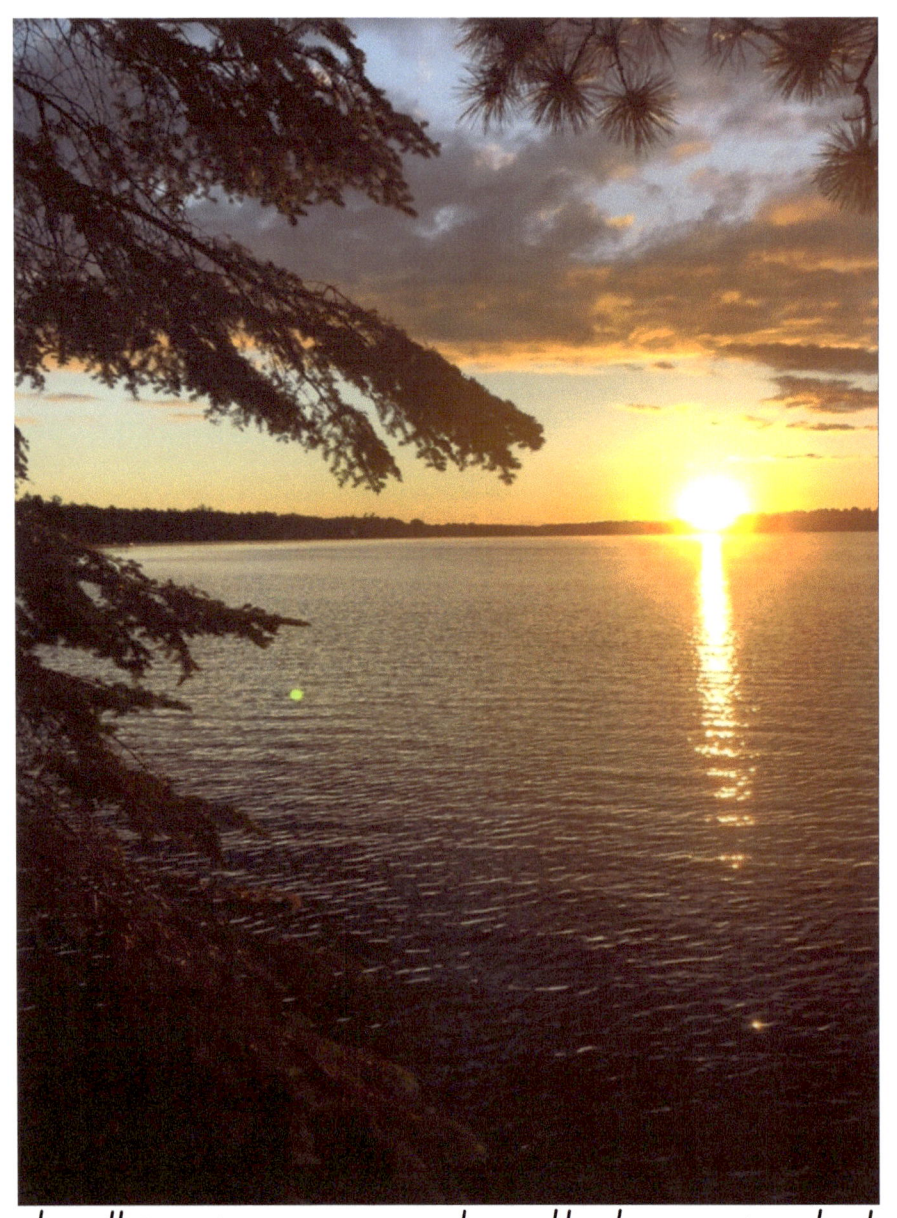

...that will inspire new wonders that promise to begin.

www.ingramcontent.com/pod-product-compliance
Lightning Source LLC
Chambersburg PA
CBHW041935240526
45473CB00034B/1703